Participation

Falling in Love with Reality

Participation:
Falling in Love with Reality

Copyright © 2018 Jeff Brunson
Cover Photo: Anna K. Brunson

All rights reserved. No part of this book may be used or reproduced in any manner whatsoever without written permission except in the case of brief quotations embodied in critical articles and reviews.

Printed in the United States of America

ISBN: 978-1724586346

Jeff Brunson's Writing,
A Flow through the Years of His Work
(with the *Desire & Intent* of Participation)

*Wading the Stream of Awareness:
The Building of a Confident Leader*

Jeff's *desire* drives him to encourage your Trueness, as you know that what you need, you have, already inside.

*The Rhythm of Trueness:
A Poetic Journey for the Leader Within*

*In the Middle with Trueness:
The Transforming Resonance of a Leader*

Jeff is committed to assisting your Trueness in all you do; where you discover that moving consciously to the *middle* is a power strategy founded in Love, a Love present from the start.

*The World Needs You:
Selected Verse; Contemplation, Poetry, Love*

Participation: Falling in Love with Reality

Jeff's *intent* draws him into a commitment of support, opening you to the impact of your Trueness as you lead and guide others toward wholeness.

Each book referenced above is available on Amazon.com

Participation

Falling in Love with Reality

Jeff Brunson

Contents

Part I   Wade

The Call into the Rhythm of Contemplation & Flow
Page 7

Part II   Walk

The Call into the Middle with Poetry & Encounter
Page 33

Part III   Wonder

The Call into the Unfolding of Love & Oneness
Page 59

Index of Poems
Page 81

Trueness

*Who one is
since the beginning
is already present,
with colors and hues on an original palette,
simply waiting to be stroked
into present being
by the dance and dialogue
of artist and canvas.*

Welcome
to
The Work of Trueness

Falling in love with reality is ultimately falling in love with Trueness itself. To fall in love with your own Trueness, and that of others, is to create the connection with the oneness that already exists within the reality of love.

When Trueness finally supersedes divided thinking, you are now in loving participation with life and living.

The energy for your participation, and therefore impact, lives within a unique love given in the beginning, flowing from a specific voice, designed.

Wade in this Truth.

Passion and purpose join and shimmer in bright presence, only as you allow. The courage to let go is fundamental to the language of resonance—freeing your voice of love in a needy world.

Walk with this Truth.

Trueness will deliver intended impact when you hold in your own loving hands the reality of you since the beginning. For in this reality, you can now feel, hear, and see with the clarity of faith, hope, and love.

Wonder at this Truth.

From the Beginning

Love is where I came from,
and love is where I'll return.
In-between, intended it was,
love meant to guide and lead.
In reality love always did,
sadly, I didn't always listen.
But now, blessed opportunity
and gift of awareness, I
can hear the voice of love
in everything I see–
but aware I must remain,
Wading
Walking
Wondering.
It's my time to live,
live according
to the Trueness
given me
from the beginning.

Part I

Wade

Contemplation & Flow
To experience something gladly,
paying attention with love

The Call into the Rhythm of Contemplation & Flow

Trueness will call at you until you pay attention. Trueness is not a persistent partner calling out for you to dance. Trueness is the dance, where you are wholly alive in reality.

Trueness demanded I step into the flow and pay attention. And attention captured, rhythm was delivered into continually deeper, truer passion and participation. Participation requires courage, and the courage you need to wade into the flow is encoded within your Trueness. Without such original courage you are completely open to the lies of expectation, a set of false standards determined to move you well beyond the reach of your Trueness and its rhythm.

The rhythm of my own Trueness has called me into a work with varying expressions, each spoken from the voice given me since the beginning. It is through these expressions, and maybe because of them, that my rhythm was washed into the open.

In my work, I focus on individual leaders. Consequent of this focus, my writing continually takes me into the stories of these individuals, where each is learning to wade in the awareness of the true self.

Contemplation, Poetry, and Love: Flow, Encounter, and Oneness: All words seemingly esoteric and spiritual. But esoteric and spiritual doesn't mean that they are not real. Quite the contrary, to only believe in one side of the river over another is unreal, allowing lies that keep you from knowing the reality of the flow.

I talk, and write, about applying the true self in work, and practicing from this original source, because it is what I know. Working full time one spends around two thirds of the waking life in this thing called work. So, as best as one can, why not make it as good as it can possibly be? Why not free both desire and intent into the middle of the flow of Trueness?

With the strength of voice given since the beginning, and the freedom found by stepping into the middle of the flow, hold the pearl of great price, your Trueness.

Simplicity, Reality, and Love

I just want to step in
and Wade.

I only want to be steady
and quiet
in my Walk.

I want to hear and know
Oneness as I allow into my life
Wonder–at the smallest,
simplest, and so very important things
of an everyday life.

It was the middle of October, waiting for the color, and I was in my new favorite coffee shop thinking on this next series of writing. I began to soak in a joy I felt, while resisting any temptation to stray away from the depth I sensed in the stream of life and living.

I had just released my fourth book, which is a book of selected verse encouraged out of the depths by my beautiful friend, editor, and publisher. Do I have yet another book in me? I think so, maybe more than just one. Parker J. Palmer talks of being one of those writers who only has one book in him, but he continues writing about the topic in varying expressions. I feel this as well. And like Palmer, I don't seem to mind.

I'm a simple person I suppose. It could seem I don't like challenge, not writing multiple books on varying topics, but it is very challenging to write about the one topic providentially placed in my very soul. This topic doesn't define me; rather it is a wonderful energy force in my soul–this thing I know as Trueness.

Wade–Walk–Wonder
Why this alliteration? As my soul sister Pam said, it has a flow inherent. And as she knows from her encouragement of me, I am captivated by flow, and the rhythm it washes into the open.

It begins in the Wade. I step into life and living freed from the lie of any single expectation. Forgiving everything, gently placing all in the flow, allows me to step out and Walk in the beauty of it all–all that is reality. In the steadiness of such walking, I am deeply encouraged by how it all fits together (how it can all work together for good, if I only allow it to do so). Then, at some point I begin to actually see an unfolding; and this is the Wonder.

In this day and time, I find it sad when we allow ourselves to not be filled with wonder. We believe we are well informed, that we see and understand so much. All that, to me, gets in the way of real wonder.

Contemplation, Poetry, Love; words shared by Dan, a dear friend and brother in spirit. With these words he captured a rhythm representative of our longstanding friendship and honest, soulful conversations.

Flow, Encounter, Oneness; words that have joined the above rhythm as I've explored more fully my own Trueness, while also helping others come to know Trueness as the power for self-love and love in leadership.

In your reading of this book, my desire is that you find deep encouragement for the pearl of great price I call Trueness. My intent is that, as you embrace this power, you will grow in loving leadership, helping others know the need for true self to be confidently present in all one does.

It is not so much the world that we need to understand; it is ourselves, our true self. You've heard it said, it's not the destination that's so important, it's the journey; and that definitely applies here. This is the reason I decided to write in the flow of Wade–Walk–Wonder.

Enjoy the journey into and with Trueness.

Contemplation & Flow

Am I a contemplative? I have always been one inclined to spend much time in introspective thought, maybe more than needed for my own good (an Achilles' heel of needing to understand things). My mother on more than one occasion said, "You think too much." Strictly defined, contemplation is a long, thoughtful look at something. I prefer Richard Rohr's version and the important added word, 'a long, *loving* look at anything.'

Whether or not I am a contemplative, I know I certainly desire to be more absorbed in life and living. What might it look like to be contemplative? The answer—at least for now, and for me—just may be in how I see contemplation itself: *It is compassion for oneself, and all, as one.* From such a stance might we become adept at feeling, hearing, and seeing in, with, and through love?

Love is a mystery in our world of work and leadership; but why? What might happen if we, as leaders, allowed love to be at the very core of each choice and every decision; allowing such energy to flow through all we do for those we lead, influence, and serve?

In the years just before writing my first book, I participated in a small, intimate writing group. During this time writing together I discovered my soul connection with Pam. She didn't just listen in what I would write, she would feel, hear, and see with me, and often deeper within than I was noticing myself. She paid attention with love.

Brought to my consciousness in my writing and expression was my consistent movement toward water, and my desire to be in and with the flow. Flow is not just some fleeting construct to me. Rather, flow is a tangible connecting of experiences through the reality and power of relationship; a landscape filled with moving reality, should one only stand still long enough to see.

And there lies the rub, the difficulty, and the self-imposed barrier to feeling, hearing, and seeing reality: a lack of stillness.

In my book, *In the Middle with Trueness*, I wrote about Christie. She is a leader who operates consistently in her preferred extroverted manner, using innate strengths given her since the beginning. When her voice of positive, open intent is guiding her, she acts from her true self and opens the space for others to participate. At one point, she needed the guidance of her own rhythm as she set her intention toward building a stronger relationship with her boss.

As I asked Christie questions to learn more about her boss, she began to tell his story, a story filled with her compassion, care, and concern. When she first told me about the troubles in this relationship, it was filled with frustrations in their interactions with each other. But as she told this story in light of her own Trueness, I listened as she began to forgive her perceptions.

Right there in her story, in the natural flow of her own voice, she discovered her tangible process to not only improve interactions, but to consciously step into the reality and power of the relationship with him. The integrity of her process was vividly supported by her willingness to be still in the story. The telling of the story blessed her with a new way of seeing, and therefore a more real way of participating.

"Perception is reality." This is a longstanding belief in our society within our work settings, and like so many clichés it has become overused in a context formed by a severe lack of understanding. Individual observation, trained in an unbalanced way of assuming, does indeed lead us in interpreting what we perceive—and this is what we then believe to be reality. This falsely formed reality only furthers our individual and collective unconsciousness to what is really transpiring.

What is really going on—to feel, hear, and see reality—requires us to simply pay attention with the mind in the heart (the mind incorporated into the flow of the heart). This requires love.

Pam helped me pay attention to where I seemed to consistently go to bring forth words, and the meaning I intended within each composition. She paid attention in each scene where I painted with words and with my energy. Thus, flow led me to consider the meaning and the encounter with contemplation.

A Larger Cadence

Writing, in and of itself, for me has become an important form of contemplation; a long and loving look into the matter of my attention, and at the original level, my intention. At last, after much practice, I learned the power of the writing process: that it was much more than just producing some content, that there was something calling me into the depths of context, honoring experience, and thus drawing me toward more meaningful participation.

As I remain open to contemplation, what it is and how it manifests in my life and living, I am convinced it flows in diverse incarnations grounded within the reality of who we are. Does how we learn have connection with how contemplation might become part of our stillness and flow? Through experience and experimentation, we each have developed how we best learn, where, in true learning, we each have found our best methods for simply paying attention.

The integrity of Christie's process to build and maintain a more authentic relationship with her boss was undergirded by the power she found in paying attention, leveraging her own rhythm to wade the flow. As she learned, no matter the issue or challenge, it can be placed in the flow. Whatever is placed in the flow will be free to do what is good and right down stream, whether this is seen or not by the one who acts from Trueness.

This, from my experience, I know, if an individual acts from Trueness—living her or his own rhythm—then this person is a leader. Our world so needs this leadership to come alive in each person, as much as possible.

Rhythm and Attention
Whatever contemplative stance I might envision for myself, I know such seeing becomes gracefully clearer as I move closer to my Trueness—deeply honoring the rhythm given to me. In volume five of

my work journaling, I asked myself this question; "What is it about rhythm I so desire to teach?"

The deep context of this work I do has led me deeper into my own Trueness. I am recognizing a need to share, more often and ever more deeply, the abundance available through becoming aware of your rhythm, and more consistently choosing in the cadence of such beautiful simplicity and truth.

I teach about rhythm because I want you to know the journey makes sense, as it is traveled, with conscious presence. I teach rhythm so you can be aware, focused, and loving on your journey, and in the larger cadence. I teach rhythm so you may lead in a needy world—leading from the authentic rhythm given you since the beginning. I teach rhythm as a way to teach love—love *for* your work and love *in* your work—and how such love is profitable, not a business strategy but a way of living Trueness, embracing the larger cadence of contemplation, poetry, and love.

The true leaders I've known draw their energy from the story of a larger cadence. They are learning to lead in the tension of the middle, where they assume, within their own Trueness, the risk of balancing the collision of proactivity and reactivity in our all too prevalent reactive cultures.

Recently, with the intent to encourage, I reached out to some leaders and shared something I had read that was fitting to knowing and leveraging this balancing act. Here is part of the response sent by one leader:

> "I was just talking last week with my friend about how you balance accountability and ownership without personal identification with the outcome that affects your non-work life negatively—the test being—can you relate to your family and

friends in the same way if you're blowing your plan out OR behind in the month by $1M?

"Getting back into a sales role, I'm working on finding that place. Some days I'm closer to that goal than others. Any advice?"

I shared with him what I've learned, and believe, that there should not be any separation between what we do and who we are—which of course translates into: There should not be any difference in How we do things and Who we are—the true self.

In an atmosphere driven mostly by outcomes (reactive), it makes it difficult to operate from authenticity (proactive) on a regular basis. The thing that so many fail to recognize is that it's not either/or, but both/and.

Instead of allowing the work life to affect non-work life, what if we turned that around? So many times working one-on-one with a leader, they take me into something personal. I don't go there on my own, but if invited in, I oblige them. A good example would be communicating better with a spouse or a teenage child. I tell individuals that if they can meet these kind of challenges in the ever so important, and depth, of personal life, doing so in the workplace is a cinch.

So how does all this relate to being in a sales role, or any other business role? Think about it. I believe it does. It has for me. But what do you think?

I know this; when I approach someone from my own Trueness, keeping my commitment to do what is good and right for me to do (and letting that go to do its thing), and doing it from a personal voice of Love and Encouragement (my voice and the strength of my voice), good things happen. I find myself worrying less about the numbers—because the outcomes do take care of themselves.

It takes a measure of confidence to see past the distractions in one's everyday and focus the energy of Trueness. It seems there are many reasons for a lack of attentiveness in our daily lives, supposed reasons that simply become excuses to not pay attention. If we don't wade into Trueness, we lose the opportunity for connectedness, with each other and with all things. But stepping into the stream of who we really are, we can begin a loving and conscious flow toward oneness.

> *"To be true is to flow, and in the flow one experiences both freedom and obstacle. Our own unique rhythm is moved to fullness by the notes and cadences of our own song, and finding harmony in a larger composition."*
> –from *The World Needs You*, Second Contemplation

Reality, what is it? Answering this could, I'm sure, fill volumes. But for the purposes of falling in love with it, reality is somewhere in the realm of letting go. Letting go is not about a lack of caring, but simply about not having the need to grasp at things, in a manner where holding on is damaging to self and others. Letting go, we learn to see within the unfolding of it all.

And Now ...

Important it is
to breathe in grace
each morning,
to feel living grace
as reality.

For into graceful flow entering,
I begin to hear resonance, given me
since the beginning; reminded
that such voice is closer to reality,
the truth of who I am, the pulse
between soul and spirit.

Blessed then, my eyes to see
more clearly in the oneness,
the story of which I am a small part;
a part nonetheless,
and often without even knowing so,
an important part to one ...

The threads of reality, seen through
the clear lens of movement, weave
for the one seeing
a depiction of belonging.

In such flow is grace,
blessed connection from
what is, now.

Wading into Trueness

Trueness is the deeper context to which this work has led me; a work to which I've been led and now find pulling me forward.

One's journey toward, and with, Trueness begins with the Wade, the choice to participate—even well before we understand all we feel, hear, and see flowing around us. I have come to a place in my life and living where I consider all my efforts to be *The Work of Trueness*.

I believe that the true self is not lost *out there* but buried *in here*. I also believe it is one's life-long work to uncover and live from this Trueness. Our Trueness is the pearl of great price buried in that field, the ground we purchase by letting go of all that is false and in the way of the flow of our voice, a brand of resonant love uniquely given to us from the beginning.

At the core of the nature of reality is paradox. We are being unrealistic when, in our life and living, we constantly need to separate; to make choices and decisions loosely structured on the lies of dualistic thought. And the most serious flaw at reality's core is the failure to embrace as *one* the human and divine. It seems to me that any subsequent refusal to hold any other true paradox is built on this failure.

Do You Hear?
The most important tool in the craft of my work is that of listening. My very desire and intent in this work depends on the attention I give in listening. Listening is the tool, but really hearing another is the skill (art). To allow the two to properly work together, I must get myself out of the way.

I've found that most people don't listen well to themselves, and therefore not hearing profound points of resonance from both inner and outer charges; the impact of desire and intent. Several years ago I fell victim to my own lack of hearing.

I was having an economically challenging year, telling myself a story of betrayal and evaporating value of this work in which I had become so invested. During this time, two dear friends encouraged me to listen to what my clients said to me about our work together, and to really hear in their words the impact for them in the intersection of my own desire and intent.

Providentially timed with this encouragement (and because of it), I found myself in a conversation with Amy, a wonderful client and supporter of my work through the years. Sensing my walk along the cliff-edge of depression, she lovingly took me to task for not intuitively knowing the value of the work I do, and what I had done for so many. She decided to speak for them.

Speaking to my own gifted rhythm, she said:
- *We learn from you and take this to others, proliferating our mentorship.*
- *You teach us how to leverage our relationships.*
- *You give us skills to teach the methodology to others in order to improve both individual and organizational impact.*

Needless to say, I've kept Amy's words before me in the years since receiving them from her faithful courage. This beautiful, blessed interaction with her helped pull my steps away from a desperate edge and inspirited my walk back into my own cadence. Amy knew my rhythm because she had become conscious of her own rhythm in the experience of being truly heard.

Forgiving Reality
In my book, *The Rhythm of Trueness*, I share the rhythmic flow gifted to my consciousness through my study of Fr. Richard Rohr's writing: Forgive Everything / Everything Belongs / See the Unfolding.

It is in the Wade, stepping into life and living, freeing oneself from the lies of expectations, where we are struck with the paradox of stillness and flow. In the flow, sudden awareness of things moving together with or without us, we realize the importance of our participation. But to move such realization into active engagement, partaking of the energy available to us, we must let go of the false standards that have so far defined us.

To *forgive everything* is only possible somewhere in the intersection of forgiving reality and forgiving yourself for the reality created by circumstances, and any set of standards by which you may have been taught and most likely controlled. To forgive reality, as one knows it, is the proclamation of true freedom, and forgiving self is the freedom to be true.

Forgive Everything

The Beginning; I often refer to this phrase of measure, as in, *since the beginning, from the beginning,* etc. I do this as a matter of encouragement, saying to you that what you most need is already present within. My propensity to *encourage* is an example of something within me endowed since the beginning. Anytime I include such phraseology, I am referring to the powerful simplicity of present grace.

I want to tell you about my brother. To begin, I share a somewhat incomplete poem, composed on a long walk as I thought about him. It is incomplete in my mind as it relates to its inadequacy in speaking to the reality and grace of this man.

A brother I have,
father and mother
a shared bond.
Deeply I trust,
even deeper I respect
this brother in blood.

Trust and respect I give,
but earned both are.

It's true, I suppose,
that over time
what you say
and what you do
come together in truth.

A powerful thing it is to say
a wonderful thing it is to claim
I trust your truth.

This attempt of putting words to what I know of this man came in the year after his daughter Molly's death. Molly was the most courageous person I have ever known, and her spirit was bright, loving, and compassionate for all others. And right there in paradoxical courage with her were her mom and her dad.

In spite of medical prediction, Molly made it beyond her 39th year (she was the longest-living liver transplant recipient at the time of her death). Those years were brutal to her body. When I consider such reality as the perpetual sickness of the entire life of a child, I am sadly amazed at the ease with which we humans give our energy to the insignificant; things in life and work made dreadfully significant by our false belief that we can exert control. Such belief is unreal, because it is formed in the space of false expectation: untruth we too freely allow as we compulsively grasp at things.

In the last months of our mom's life, my brother and I worked together around key components of securing credible care for her, most of which fell under his watchful eye, which was a loving duty well beyond just his geographical closeness to her. Being personalities of very different preferences and gifts, we worked well together in the processes required for mom's care. I have been privileged through the years to be inspired by the grace of my brother's strength.

It is a graceful privilege to know someone for many years. My brother is four years my senior. We therefore didn't do a lot of things together growing up. I do remember a lot of front yard wiffle ball games; totally played within his situational rulebook to assure his victory! We were both in our thirties when we became close, spending quality time fishing, allowing us both to find respite from some parts and parcels of reality.

My brother and sister-in-law are, as they say, tough as nails. They have had to be, for the sake of all their children. They have both come to forgive reality. If it were not so I would not see the generosity and love that flow through them. Molly's love and compassion was learned from her parents as well as gifted to her since the beginning. And she too was tough as nails.

Here is what I know: My brother is true, and for this he makes no apology. I'm not referring to opinions or any other superfluous views. I know his Trueness. I have seen its steadfastness all my life. His wade through both joy and suffering has washed him onto a path where he contemplatively walks. This is what I know, the grace of this man.

I hope I never stop experiencing, never stop learning, and never stop growing. For in the experiencing, learning, and growing, I am washed into the open with each encounter. In this openness passion can flow. I can wade, walk, and wonder with the passion paradox of joy and suffering; held, released, and spoken in the poetry of Trueness.

To get to what has been present, within you, *since the beginning,* it is critical to learn the tenacious call to forgive reality, to *forgive everything.* And as you find yourself evolving within, you will see yourself acting in new ways, ways more attuned *by* Trueness.

Washed into the Open

The journey of learning,
experientially,
road without end, reality.
To forgive such, necessary
for the sake of flow;
limitless, uninhibited freedom.

Experience is a teacher.
But do we learn?
Rhythm, the acquisition,
the purchase of mastery
with the currency given
since our beginning.

Yet, what do we master?
Surely not others,
probably not ourselves.
The mastery, less about expertise,
more about tireless contemplation;
compassion for oneself,
and all,
as One.

And within contemplative freedom
we learn
to walk
in the cadence
of simplicity and truth,
the reality of our own currency,
our poetry and our love.

Realness, buried under the sediment
of expectation.
Spirit, attentive to the strokes
of Trueness,
sluicing deposits of limitation.

And, stepping
into the stream
of who we really are,
we are washed into the open,
delivered yet again onto
our own path.

Part II

Walk

Poetry & Encounter
A cadence of experience, a rhythm of expression
formed by graceful attentiveness

The Call into the Middle with Poetry & Encounter

Trueness calls us to evolve openly throughout our journey. We evolve truly not by doing things differently, but by doing different things; contemplating and acting from our experience and encounter.

The way of being true is in the middle. When I speak of the middle I naturally include leadership in the meaning. The middle is not a place, or even an attitude. Rather, it is freedom implanted in Trueness. From the middle we grow in the ability to release the wish for a different reality. Our experience in *forgive everything* is opening us to the belonging that is critical to our learning to flow in the reality of the true self. This is the freedom implanted in Trueness.

I am in the middle of work with leaders because true leadership flows through an individual who is:

- ❖ Contemplative—embracing the Trueness guiding one's Wade
- ❖ Poetic—trusting the Trueness strengthening one's Walk
- ❖ Loving—seeing through Trueness the blessed Wonder

Standing to one side, denigrating the other, it becomes impossible to pay attention with love. You may love those who agree with you, and kowtow to your narcissistic stance, but you have gained nothing. And, you've given nothing.

Your true self is your poetic presence, the resonance of your reality. Within this reality is your freedom to contemplate and act on what is good and right for you to do. Trueness leads you to the middle of self, a blessed jewel present from the beginning. Now you can bring Trueness vividly to the middle of each encounter. Creating such steadiness in your walk is attention magnified by grace, and reality clearing a path for participation. Participation begins within, and we must grow and transform individually if there is to be any real participation together.

Your rhythm of Trueness is your art. You must trust your rhythm for the sake of the impact you are meant to have in this needy world. In the middle, the inspiring reality of your Trueness, you lead us to allow our differences to blend and belong, bringing us together into reality and participation.

Trueness Meets the World

To walk, in a world of paths,
along one's own path,
a paradox in the making,
of focus and distraction,
choice and decision,
of what's inside
meeting what's outside.

Truth, no matter the origin,
pulls one inwardly
into the truth of self,
spirit true, since the beginning.

Truth, doing its work within,
pushes one out, a self
openly evolving, a path
providentially unfolding.

I know I'm privileged to work with many wonderful individuals, and I also know the value reaped from the observations and wisdom of these spirits. From these leaders I often hear about the belief that people, in general and for the most part, do not go into the workplace to do a bad job. Rather, each consciously or unconsciously wishes to operate from their true self, to add value from his/her own way of being, and to serve some larger transformative purpose. Such wise observation is an example of an individual leader's grasp of *Everything Belongs*.

Kevin is one of those wonderful, wise individuals. There have been significant changes in his organization, changes thrusting everyone into transition. In a conversation about change and organizational culture, Kevin pointed out that the components of an evolving culture are not linear; the actions to build and maintain a healthy culture must happen simultaneously, working together for good.

And so it is within the flow of Forgive Everything / Everything Belongs / See the Unfolding. It is not necessarily a linear flow. It is a very interactive relationship. However, like many things of both mind *and* heart, it helps to at least begin by seeing the linear flow, and to then allow it to move toward relationship.

Deep into the work Kevin and I were doing together, we reached the point in my methodology where we compose an objective to tangibly focus Trueness into conscious application and practice. In the session following the creation of his objective, and after time he spent reflecting on its flow, Kevin acknowledged its resonance, stating that it represented his rhythm and true self. As we reviewed the objective together, I pointed out the energy drawn from the three things he wanted from our work; three things he had wisely stated in our very first session.

Kevin knows that changes are part and parcel to each transition. He also knows that transitions build one upon another to support transformation, and that collective transformation can only happen when, as individuals, we participate together in a way of being true.

"Being transformative is a constant state, like being a leader." –Kevin

Now more conscious of his own rhythm, Kevin is focusing his Trueness into the presence of others and their way of being. He has taken accountability to break down his own mental constructs and constraints, stepping into the middle of the flow without any need to separate and divide, furthering and freeing his way of being as a transformational leader. The impact of Kevin's Trueness, made real by his choices, decisions, and actions, depends on the attention he gives to his relationship with the flow—his own rhythm and the flow of a larger purpose.

We break from reality, and our own Trueness, when we step out of the middle, and the flow, not onto our own path and the walk, but to a divisive, separating position to one side or the other. Kevin may not claim so, but I see him as a contemplative leader. Contemplation and a non-divisive spirit, these make Kevin the transformational leader that he is.

As part of what he desires and intends for those he leads, Kevin is attached to the drive to help others be successful, and must let go (not grasp at) what he intends, that everyone feels like a valuable member of the whole. And right in the middle, his Trueness meets the world as he leads from his voice of *Honesty*, paying attention with his brand of leadership love.

Kevin's objective for application and practice in Trueness reads as follows:

> I Actively Support an Environment Where We Develop People

- Clarity: Leading a Unified Team—I look for obstacles in the way of our individual and mutual success, and then lead us into a dialogue that delivers us into unification.
- Listen: Being Available Throughout the Organization—I know that, basically, everyone wants to do a good job, and people need someone to help them get there – this is in their control even if they do not realize it.
- Alignment: Helping Others Cooperate, Collaborate, & Contribute—most problems have somewhere in the root cause a lack of communication – people need to like what they do, and this brand of alignment helps the individual be successful, happy, and part of a team.

Kevin's desire and intent form the foundation upon which he builds his attention for loving leadership. This is the energy for his walk and the opening to his poetry and encounter.

Poetry & Encounter

I write poems. I try not to think too much about whether or not I'm good at doing so. To me, a poem is simply a response to an encounter, a rhythmic expression waiting for its encounter.

When writing, I quite often pause to wait for a story to tell, opening me further to my own voice in the composing. Sometimes the stories are from my own experience, but mostly they flow from my experience of another. The experience of another is an encounter with the human paradox, the counterintuitive realities that make life and living worth the attention.

An encounter is a confrontation only when one allows it to be.

The paradoxical quality of encounter is that, although unexpected, it is conflict neutral–an unconstrained, holding together of what we as humans have learned to judge as opposites. Judging within duality dams the flow of one's voice.

Ericka is a caring, focused, intelligent executive. She is capable of quick, creative, and detailed analysis, and can consequently make decisions in short order. However, her voice of *Trust* is calling her into deeper presence with others for the sake of more meaningful interaction in a space of creative contribution. She desires for others the reward and fulfillment that come with thinking critically in the midst of our encounters with change and challenge. She leads others into a conflict neutral interval between analysis and action. This is Ericka's due diligence as a leader, her voice flowing.

An encounter is a lesson in reality, and a true paradox. Consider a meeting of two individuals, obviously different from one another. While common cultural observation may have us trained to perceive our differences, failure to recognize differences may be precisely what keeps us from oneness.

I've worked with many people who have expressed the desire to collaborate at both deeper and broader levels. What I've learned, especially through my own flailing experience, is that we miss true collaboration and unity because we communicate too regularly from our own context; our own set of preferences both internally and externally. Failing to see the differences between myself and the other person keeps me from seeing past each variance and into the individual's Trueness, and keeps me from bringing my own Trueness more vividly into the reality and beauty of the encounter.

Reality is infinite. Our thinking is too often finite.
Over the last several years my wife and I have been actively simplifying life and living: working from attic down to rid ourselves of things packed away or no longer needed, selling that property, leasing a down-sized space for two years, then buying a similar space closer to our daughter. Well enough into this process I now ask myself what this detachment is all about.

It began with simplification in mind; we have moved in great strides toward this goal. We have let go of many things, and we still have a bit to do to let go of the need for some other things. However, at this point, I am realizing the goal was less about simplification, or even detaching from things, and more about removing what is in the way of knowing Trueness, and knowing the reality of oneness.

Now that we have more freedom, we detach from things to actually learn to detach from any part of self not indicative of Trueness. These parts of us are not necessarily bad per se; they simply are no longer in control. The obstacles to Trueness are never outside of us. We become the barrier by attaching our worth, in any way, to things external to our true self, expecting these things to define us, or even help in marking out the fullness of our reality.

We are not complete as contemplative leaders unless our contemplation is shared. The answer to how it is shared and what sharing looks like is found in compassion, for oneself, and all, as one.

Erika's compassion is rooted in how she shares from her voice of trust. When sharing from her voice, she instinctively serves the other by contributing and helping in whatever way she can in the moment. This is contemplation in action. This is what Ericka cannot help but do when voice is freely flowing between her and the other.

Ericka's conscious attention is being applied to her encounters for reasons important to her and to those who depend on her. The more she works from her own Trueness the more she draws true contribution from others toward possibility and potential.

The love and care that others deserve, flows through us to them. If Ericka only communicated and acted from her own context, the world would miss out on the beautiful influence of her brand of love. Thankfully, she is giving her attention with her true self, thus freeing energy in leading others into more rewarding participation.

The contemplative leader's love is real, because love is reality.

Graceful Attentiveness

Like encounter, reality is conflict neutral. You may have heard it said, in response to some situation or another; "It is what it is." This is often said in resignation, a throwing up of the spiritual hands as one gives up totally, or it can be a simple acceptance of what is, in the moment. A peaceful center can accept reality. It is not giving up or giving in. Rather, it is one's attention magnified by grace.

In conversation with a friend, Ericka was sharing about our work together, and about what she was learning about herself. Her friend made a statement about a particular personality profile, sharing her type and stating that she and Ericka were just alike. The truth is, Ericka's profile and her friend's profile are completely different.

Her friend is more on the introverted side of things, gives great energy to process and detail, and tends more toward perfectionism, doing things in the right way. Ericka is more extraverted, direct, decisive, and clear, driven to get the right things done. The friend sees Ericka similar to herself because of grace; Ericka's energy focused on this core relationship and loving her friend as she centers the best of who they both are individually and together.

I can only imagine how this friend looks forward with eagerness to being in Ericka's graceful presence, their differences coming together and belonging.

The Lie of Expectation
It is quite embarrassing as I think about it, how often I allow some expectation to tell me a lie. I'm not referring to a presupposition imposed from some external source. I've become rather skilled at silencing those. More so, I point toward a self-inflicted conjecture that strays from reality.

To pay attention void of grace is to tell oneself a lie.

In the Petri dish of falsity, internal violence can develop in the cultures of false expectation, judgment, and comparison. When left too long to culture, and then uncovered, the spoiled combination spreads infected messages that have nothing to do with who one is in reality.

When I launched out on my own in this work that called me, I entered with a piece of expectation-baggage; anyone in this line of work must publish a book, and quickly. So, as I thought authors do, I committed time early in the morning and began to write. This expectation, with its falsity tormenting my thinking, led me through two false starts in attempting to create a manuscript. Later, upon finding my voice and my own writing process, I looked back on what had been written during those mornings. It was useless to what I was then composing in-voice, but quite necessary in getting me to that point.

When I find a wonderful writer, I read a lot of what he or she writes. While I love studying style in these skilled writers, I know I've had to find my own way; my own rhythm with pen and page that allows my voice flow in composing. I consequently let go of the goal of being an *author* and embraced the diligent duty of being a *writer*.

The Truth of Grace
I begin most mornings with my journal. Quite often in that time I find myself simply sitting in gratitude. Is gratitude part of grace, or at least a mark of grace? I think so. And grace is much more free to flow the more I can stay on the path with my walk.

At one point in my journaling, I found myself expressing a need to be validated as a writer. At first it was unclear as to the source of this expressed need. Then it was time to write about the lie of expectation. It then occurred to me that I was again allowing some expectation, or set of expectations, to pronounce a wholesale judgment on me as a writer.

Four books later, and this one in progress, my methodology is still evolving and teaching me in the process. It took much practice, pain, and persistence to clear my thinking and free the writer I am. My journaling assured me that I am the writer I'm intended to be, and the same practice, pain, and persistence will continue with only the objective of making me better at the craft.

If we are not careful to take guard against false expectations, we will stray from our path and allow damaging interruption to the steadiness of our walk. To know *everything belongs* is to have come to a confident stand, and to know a more secure and steady walk on our own path. It becomes a way of being with reality, of being less distracted by any particular want of a reality other than the one we have. Wanting a reality other than the one in front of us can freeze us in a moment of real need and keep us from doing what is good and right to do in the reality of unique encounter.

Grace and gratitude make you stronger. Freedom is nourished by the acknowledgement of specific blessings in your walk. A litany of gratitude helps you remain aware of life and living as good things gather and unfold–and this is grace. The confidence needed for traveling the path is increased by consciously consistent praise for every event and connection.

Gratitude and grace are marks of a contemplative leader. This leader can confidently stand in the middle, see things without a need to separate and judge, and walk steadily with the staff of reality; blessed by the wonders expressed in the truth of poetry and the experience of encounter.

Unconjectured

Stepping from life into living,
from internal to external,
soul flowing toward others.

Stepping from life into living,
deeply encouraged
by the fitting together,
all things working together
for good, if but allowed.

From expectation to graceful anticipation,
Trueness navigating turn and toil.

Seeing past falsity
and into the soul,
courage grows in each encounter,
holding the paradox of being
human and divine.

Reality clears a path,
a way of being true.

Attention now given,
grace within relationship,
grace within the flow.

The Path

"They're just living their lives." A wise colleague said this in response to a frustration. Unfortunately, I was the holder of that frustration. Along with the Achilles' heel of needing to understand things at a too often intense level, there is yet another one; I also hate to be ignored. Let me walk into a restaurant, be ignored, and I'll walk out never to return. Sorry, it is what it is. During the challenging year in which my colleague spoke this, I was feeling ignored. It was frustration built up from unnecessary expectations I had set for others as I was attempting to control things in the flow.

At the core of life and living is what it means to walk. To participate is to step from life into living. Life is observation. Living is participation. Life is the energy of internal focus. Living is the energy of external focus. Life is the birth of new ideas and creative, intuitive ways of being. Living is the freeing of such energy into a needy world, as we do what is good and right for us to do along our own path.

My colleague's comment got my attention, brought me to ground. I was embarrassed by the intensity with which I had succumbed to those false expectations; scripts written that had nothing to do with reality. I had strayed from rhythm, the cadence of my own way of being in this work I do.

Somehow in my journey, three strengths have evolved and joined together to give me, not only a rhythm in the work, but a mode for doing the work: Gather-Give-Grow. Study has served my life and work. In study, I gather information on the one hand. On the other hand is the need to grow something with what has been gathered. When the hand of gather joins the hand of grow, I then know how to truly give. And giving is done in a steady walk, on the path with purpose.

In the beautiful tension between gather and grow, wade and wonder, I walk confidently when I give from my best self. When each encounter is met with Trueness, poetry is written in the fitting together of your desire and intent; the verse of who you are, read by another, in the impact you've made with your own life and living.

The Rhythm of Paradox

There is this,
There is that,
And the two together
I hold.
A tension of life,
A blessing for living.

As I sat in the quiet of an early Wednesday morning, the blessings of life and living were swirling about me. I pray I have had the impact upon others that is spoken in my own statement of *Desire & Intent:*

That you lovingly lead others to their own authentic confidence; as you embrace the power of who you are, and act on this Trueness.

This is a good and noble thing for me, because the collision of desire and intent were given to me; implanted from the beginning. As such, this is life, given for living. This statement doesn't define me, it was given for the defining, reality brought to my life and living.

I use the term *life and living* as a reference to one's path and to express the flow of internal to external, and open awareness to the path—the middle tension created by the paradox of life *and* living. For some, energy given to the doing helps develop awareness of being. For some, energy given to being helps develop more conscious application in the doing. It doesn't matter where one must begin, based on her or his makeup; it only matters when both are held in the blessing of creative tension, rhythm, and flow.

I speak about flow and rhythm as if they are the same thing. They are, and they are not. I speak of flow in the larger sense, that of which we are all a part. I speak of rhythm in a personal manner, that cadence within, given since the beginning, and key to knowing how we join the flow.

Dave is a natural storyteller. He leads with story, a commitment to the priority of *why*. He keeps others *in* the story in the everyday reality of a busy work life. In the flurry of implementation and execution, he helps each individual see the value of any desired direction, and possible consequent action; further encouraging the paradox of being/doing.

Dave's leadership in and with the story is balanced by his stand that *what* is for the mind and *why* is for the heart (his understanding and application of the mind incorporated into the flow of the heart). He knows it is both/and for people to be engaged. Whether it is pulling us together in and by the story, or modeling for us how to collaborate in the story, it is the generosity of leaders like Dave that draws us in and then out.

Encouraged by the Fitting Together
In my work with individual leaders, I have for years engaged in dialogue about strengths. I include this focus on each person's strengths because of a concentration in our work environments to leverage varying instruments to show people their strengths. Seeing leadership development with only the business lens, we assume a focus on strengths is telling the individual something of deep, internal truth about who they are. Rather, we are only pointing to an example of how they show up in the world, not why they show up.

This work in the external can go only so far in being of assistance to true impact. If one only lives actively from external sources, there is no flow, and there is no rhythm. Flow and rhythm are not propositions of either/or, but the holding together of both/and. The fitting together of it all, part of the energy of *everything belongs*, is part of a reality that is in our midst in this 21st Century. The fitting together is part of the attitude of true leadership.

Personally, if I try to understand this fitting together, I ultimately limit my seeing. But if I simply allow it to encourage me, I stand a much better chance at seeing how it comes together. I must not allow any need to understand, or any other Achilles' heel, to prevent me from knowing this belonging.

After many years holding the need to understand (a private version of control), I'm learning to release into what it means to contemplate and participate in the unfolding flow; taking a long, loving look at reality. Critical to this learning is remaining connected in the flow with my own rhythm.

The encouragement we need comes from within, as our desire becomes fueled by our voice and joins intention, creating the energy needed for impact.

Everything Belongs

At first, my thinking faltered and paused at great length as I tried to mentally grasp the true meaning of *everything belongs*. To say that everything belongs is *not* to say that "everything" is okay. That is clearly not a truth. Evil is still a contradiction to good, and hate is still a contradiction to love; and true contradictions are part of reality just as paradoxes—two seemingly opposing sides of one truth—are part of reality.

Many years ago, while still in the corporate world, I sat down to compose, for the first time, a life mission statement. The short version I came to at some point is, *To Love, Serve, and Understand*. It is *not* to understand first. There is for me an order and a rhythm.

Stephen Covey wrote about seeking first to understand before being understood. I agree, and for me this occurs in *love*. But when I move *understand* to the first note, by a controlling need, I break the rhythm, and understanding is no longer part of the impact of my intent. I will no longer be drawn toward my purpose, and as such I become distracted from the beautiful movement of expectation to graceful anticipation.

It was in reading Covey that I was compelled to do the work on that life mission statement. This was quite some time ago, and there's been a lot of life flowing by since then. But what I clearly remember is that once the longer version was complete, I sat down to review what had been contemplatively composed. I had typed up both versions, printed and cut to fit a nice little frame to go in my office, and sat it down on the desk in front of me to admire and review. It read as follows:

> *Although the following Statement is divided into areas, I personally do not believe that Life can be effectively divided into separations for behavior purposes. My Life is who I am at all times in all situations.*

After this opening statement, I outlined five areas as follows:

Bring into yourself by Listening and give away by Loving.

God: **Listen** to Him, and then act, in Love and obedience
Family: **Listen** to them, and then lead and act, with unconditional Love, exhortation, and strength while receiving Love and exhortation
Friends: **Listen** to them, and then act, with unconditional Love and exhortation
Others: **Listen** to the individual, and then act in service, with Love according to need guided by principle-centered living
Self: Maintain your Balance

I read through it carefully with special attention to those bullets. Suddenly I noticed that the first four bullets each began with the word, *Listen*. Suddenly I heard my own literal voice saying, "Damn, I suck at listening."

Painfully I realized that my own modus operandi with interaction was rooted in communicating mostly from my own context. Those moments with that carefully composed mission led me to make a commitment to dedicate the ensuing year to learning to become the best listener I could possibly be. All my growth and development efforts for that unfolding year were directed by that commitment. The resulting study, training, and practice fit together to transform me into a coach. My art flowed around, from, and through my newfound love of listening.

My inherent need to understand is not in itself bad, for it is a gift. When this need gets in the way it is because I allow the gift to be misplaced in the rhythm, thus converting it from gift to a want of control. Attaching mind and/or heart to any false expectation begins to distort the possibilities available within a present, graceful attentiveness. False expectations give way to unnecessary judgment and assessment that distracts attention away from our steps.

It has taken me quite a long time to open my thinking and understand the damage dualistic thinking can inflict, and it's been a journey to reduce the times I think and act from such a divisive way of seeing anything. To acknowledge and accept the totality of experience, including one's own shadow, and to learn to hold it all without the need to judge, is to know the spirit of everything belongs. Everything belongs on your path, in the context where learning and experience combine to make us better at our art.

Seeing Clearly
Remaining in the flow connected by your own rhythm is how you sustain the influence of your impact. Your impact is the story of your reach into the world, your art.

I have written about Priya before. She is a person who is energized by external focus, drawn to do then be, in the action, validated by her impact-oriented intent. As is so easy to do, she gets locked into the mode of a key strength, like getting things done, overusing the strength and therefore opening herself up to the lie of limitation that opposes the strength.

She was capitulating to the lie when she stated that she was not creative. In listening to such, she could not see the art given her, deep within, since the beginning. So from what I know of her Trueness, and hearing the truth in her words, I assembled definitions for her.

Priya's creativity, in her own words: "I'm looking for people who are thinking about the strategy of it, creating collaboration, and then executing."

Priya's art is opening the path to fullness (from her voice of Integrity), slowing down, looking at the colors on the palette available in the moment, then influencing others to both see and paint with what they have, while also creating the confidence to go after what is yet needed to complete the picture.

Spoken or unspoken, you've been given a voice, with its own unique expression. This voice calls you out and pulls you forward as you walk your path. Your voice is rhythmically freed in the mission you've been given for both personal purpose and impact in this world.

A danger found within the lie of expectation is when we create the need to know the full course of the path. The danger is real and present in the knowing. As David Whyte puts it, if you see such a path laid out clearly before you, it's probably someone else's. We deform true experience along the way by judging, assessing, separating, or trying to control anything (or anyone). All are dualistic distractions created by expectation.

You may have heard it said, when the student is ready the teacher will appear. But as the ready student, how often is the teacher appearing from within? More often than we realize, the teacher we need resides within and is one in the same as our true, creative, artistic self.

Encouraged first from inside or first from outside, in the balance of both we have courage to walk into the beauty of *everything*—all that is reality. To continue a steady walk takes internal focus and external validation, not one or the other, but both. Those energized first by internal focus are driven to be and then do what is good and right and aligned, or validated, by their desire. Those energized first by external focus are drawn to do, then be in the action in a way that is good and right and aligned, or validated, by their intent.

We know by *all* experience the power of our own Trueness, and we know through all experience the Trueness of another; but only as we know both, present since the beginning. If it weren't for the merger of my own desire and intent (creating the middle singularity of *Desire & Intent*), I could never know what it means to *see the unfolding*. I would miss the wonder of that view.

The View from Here

It is what it is,
a reality, that can only be
forgiven.

And in the forgiving
one is delivered,
invariably graced,
into one's own walk.

A desire inherent, deep within,
seeded with purpose
in the ground of Trueness,
must be encouraged
toward its intention, steadily.

And in the steadiness
of encouragement,
internally and externally,
one can hold, together
what is good, what is right,
and release voice
into the experience
of everything.

Now, one knows
by experience.
Now, one sees
through experience.

And at the pinnacle
of what is,
the view,
sweetness.

Part III

Wonder

Love & Oneness
To allow the strength of one's voice
uninhibited flow

The Call into the Unfolding of Love & Oneness

Much has been written and said about attachment and detachment. It is a mistake to see attachment and detachment as opposing forces, a polarization to be resolved. Your Trueness increases in the middle tension where desire/attachment and intent/detachment coalesce.

It is counterintuitive to think freedom increases within a space of tension. But in this tense middle, Trueness is freed and love flows out; this is the design. One's own desire and intent is a contrast of experience designed to magnify life and amplify living.

In working with the individual leader, I leverage an exercise to identify and articulate desire and intent. The resulting statement of this exercise has three rhythmic components: the drive of desire, the draw of intent, and in between a tension from which voice is amplified—if one but allows it to be so.

An individual statement of desire and intent is simply a tool for awareness of presence and conscious attention energized from the rhythm of your Trueness. In the light of articulated desire and intent, you feel, hear, and see how you are attached to the drive of desire and must actually detach from the preconceived outcome of the intent that draws you forward. When articulated from original Trueness, both desire and intent are imperative to your leadership.

The 21st Century is demanding much of us. Contrary to possible popular assumptions, these demands do not include things like doing more with less or doing more things at once. These are distractions that, remaining unaware, call us further from love and oneness that flow from our Trueness.

The demands I hear are asking us to transform individually and collectively. And in such transformation we forgive unnecessary separations as we learn to hold the tension of each teachable paradox.

My work with leadership desire and intent is a lesson in paradox, learning to hold the tension of opposing truths until you can release the resulting oneness into the flow.

Impact is assured when both being and doing flow from your Trueness, the confluence of passion, purpose, and presence.

A Heart of Wonder

Stillness,
how necessary
for our movement
in the world,
time to absorb
blessing, for the sake
of expanding.

To expand is to wonder.
To wonder is to expand.
Trueness pondered,
voice amplified,
expectations released
into the flow.

We spread, not to cover
nor overshadow.
But self to decrease
and Trueness to increase;
we then
feel the rhythm
hear the middle melody
see the impact,
and know oneness
in the experience.

Experience
places memory pins
on the track of my journey,
tying together
the privilege I've known
through the Spirits
encountered.

Oneness, a reality
difficult to grasp
without the strength
of Love.

But oneness, like it or not,
was ordained, at the beginning,
at the foundation,
at the source
of the flow.

The italicized excerpts are journaling done on a trip to the beach one year in early May, as subtropical storm Ana passed through:

> *All of nature—all-and-each-in nature—are thrilled with the sun and stillness: in the flow of life and living, even through the storm and especially now after!*
>
> *It was tempting to be angry, feel a bit cheated of sorts, at the presence of subtropical storm Ana—this prior to our departure to South Carolina. But in what I hope was trust—and simple living—we decided to leave as planned. And now I sit and write this looking at the beauty of peaceful sky, a full day ahead of what was predicted.*
>
> *It was pure blessing for us to shift our expectations to the unexpected.*

To *forgive everything* is to release our desire into the flow, and our wade in its stream. To *see the unfolding* is to trust the impact we were called to have as we observe with wonder, at the pinnacle of intent, the fitting together of it all. And right in between we walk confidently with the creative tension of *everything belongs*.

> *How necessary it is to forgive ourselves so we might love another the way they need to be loved. I am not free to love if I have not love moving freely within. Love takes over everything. That is the way it's supposed to be—the way it was designed to be.*

> *This we must believe—not in the meritocratic manner in which far too many of us have been brought up and steered about. That upbringing too I must forgive!*

Watching one scene long enough you can see the world the way it was all made to be, how it is all intended to work together. Seeing, and loving the seeing, is living.

> *The contrast ... leaving our place in the Appalachian chain to be in the strand along the Atlantic, both are wonders, alive with eternity.*

> *I of course am very glad we came on as planned in spite of uncertainty with Ana. In some strange form of experiential joy I'm very glad this storm was present at our time. Therein was a contrast of experience, a natural joy we would have missed otherwise, but the experience of which is making the privilege of being here something to gently hold.*

It is important to be purposefully peaceful as often as possible, daily, and even multiple times a day. A dedication to purposeful peace makes us more real, free in who we really are. Being purposefully peaceful does this by slowing us down in order to feel, hear, and see. Only in such vulnerable space can we hold reality while simultaneously releasing reality. This is where life and living come together.

> *Life is to be honored. And there is life beautiful all around to be observed; to be presently appreciated. And in so doing, living happens—it happens to us, as we participate in what we see.*

Blessed indeed I am. It is important now that I carry this knowing with me in every step onward. This knowing of blessedness enriches my steps and ensures kindness in how I see along the path.

> *An ocean apart ...*
>
> *I'm not currently sitting on the beach. But the thought above hit me. Looking into the seemingly eternal expanse of the Atlantic Ocean, I actually feel close to those on the other side—not separated, but joined somehow.*
>
> *I suppose I know the somehow, right? Of course I do. It's the precise same joining I know with these happy birds going about their morning.*
>
> *So joined we are. What now?*

Love & Oneness

Our unique brand of love is complete freedom, allowing us to hold opposing truths we find in life and living. These truths become more clear to us as we listen deeply. To hold is no longer about control. As we hold with the freedom love provides, we feel with wholeness, hear more succinctly, and see more clearly. You are free to be *in* and do *from* the freedom that your brand of love guarantees.

As a child I spent hours with modeling clay as a playmate. I molded short stories and full movie scripts with the consequent figures. In my teen years, in the midst of much activity with a base of life-long friends to be, I often turned down the offer of an outing to continue working on some scale model, or other project–alone.

My first memory of feeling lonely was during my last two years at the university. In those days, because the university was on a sprawling campus outside a small town, activity was often sparse on the weekend. It was one of the few weekends I stayed on campus. My home was 140 miles away and I was not long with money, cooking in my room quite often in an electric skillet with ingredients brought from home, and living the remainder on about five dollars a week (an amount giving away my age as I write this).

I walked the campus for what I remember being a few hours. I was alone and walking into loneliness. I found myself outside a small chapel. Suddenly present inside, I stood in the middle experience of alone and lonely. Such experience was a space asking me to be with what is, all that has been, all that will be–it's all now.

Nearing twenty-one years of age, about to graduate with a degree in accounting, facing an impending job search, and our upcoming wedding, it was a beautiful, settling moment, a present grounding. Forty years later, I find myself in that small chapel, metaphorically, quite often as I coach individuals and tell you some of their stories.

Surveying the years since my moment in the small campus chapel, I see how providence moved me, through experience, toward my own voice. Early on, my voice of love, and its strength of encouragement, struggled to find focus. Eventually, my voice became my focus as I translated voice into a personal, and professional, purpose and brand.

An Encounter with Voice
He was a bit older than most when he began his assignment guarding the prisoners. My guess is that Jack was more mature than most his age. He had not allowed life's realities to harden him into stone. He lived from his heart, broken open by reality, not scattered into pieces, as had sadly happened in the story of one particular prisoner.

In the ward where prisoners were placed on suicide watch, there was a particular individual who was teaching himself English by listening and searching for the right words for what he desired to translate from his native tongue. He was searching for someone to listen. Jack had walked this length of cells often and checked in on this person as the translations were being developed.

One particularly beautiful evening, the prisoner called Jack over to the cell door. He looked at Jack and pointed to a word he had written, saying, "This is my word for you." The word was *tolerance*.

The prisoner shared his story with Jack that evening. I will not share that story here. What I do share, I share because I met Jack and heard the prisoner's full story from him. The story gave insight into the teller's tragic reality, while also speaking clearly about Jack's Trueness as experienced by this prisoner.

Even before Jack and I had a chance to talk together, I was intrigued by watching Jack with his peers, his supportive eye contact and an engaging smile; a way of *being with* each person in his presence. In our one-on-one time together, I shared with Jack what I heard as he told the story of this encounter. I heard Jack's voice of love coming through, not only in the telling, but also in the very fact that such an encounter could only occur because the man in the cell chose Jack to receive his sad story.

That night, with the open door allowing the night air through, his prisoner offered a gift in exchange for being allowed to leave his story with Jack. He gave Jack the gift of awareness, letting him know the impact of his voice, and the strength of that voice, *tolerance*.

The Door to Oneness
Upon learning more about my journey, and in the process more about what both drives and draws me, my friend Judy said, "You live a true life." From this conversation, the term Trueness was given visible life in my work. My rhythm of Trueness in this work begins as I gather from desire what is needed to grow intent, and rhythm finds its full cadence as I give in the creative, tense middle space. This rhythm, authentic and true, keeps me in the flow.

When you finally commit to lead, influence, and serve from the rhythm of your Trueness, you can grasp the reality that there is no priority higher than that of your love.

In a follow up conversation with Jack, he talked about how important it is to purposefully recognize the difference between yourself and the other person in whose presence you're blessed to be. He shared other stories of stepping into that space where he carefully held what he was feeling, hearing, and seeing. It became clear to Jack, and ever more clear to me, that our voice–our individually unique brand of love–is what opens the door, and allows our differences to swirl into oneness.

In the Atmosphere of Present Being

Jack is an attentive (contemplative) leader. His loving presence is the living measure of his impact in this world, and confirmation of his willing participation in the unfolding of it all—presented to him in what he feels, hears, and sees.

To know the rhythm of *being present*, you must lovingly embrace the paradox of being both human and divine. To know the rhythm means:

> You *feel* your rhythm and open to the gratitude naturally flowing from your core.

> You *hear* the true resonance given you since the beginning, standing confidently in the middle and listening to the leader and teacher within.

> You *see* more clearly for the sake of opening further the path of impact, a crescendo of your brand of love.

In the atmosphere of *present being*, you must be willing to humbly hold the impact of your Trueness. Holding impact means:

> Forgiving your own assumptions, about self and others, freeing the flow of your voice.

> Embracing the mystery of belonging with all and everything.

> Trusting that your resonance is doing its work in the world, whether you will ever consciously know this or not.

Trusting Resonance
The month before writing this, I traveled to Chicago to facilitate a confidence building session with 50 leaders for Kevin, the executive I wrote about earlier. Our relationship goes back many years. His wife is

Amy, that loving supporter of my work for as many years. As my wife had gone with me on this trip, Amy and Kevin asked us to join them for dinner.

At the beginning of forming my coaching practice, I struggled with marketing myself. Pretty much everything I tried and did marketing-wise was both a train wreck and a waste of energy. At some point, and thanks to a couple of loving colleagues, I found my rhythm in this thing called marketing. This rhythm was found in the merger of my desire to work within the authenticity of the individual and my intent for them to be lovingly confident in their leadership.

I settled into an atmosphere of trust within my own Trueness. Simply, this is what that looks like: If I've worked with you, learning your Trueness, and I come across something while gathering, giving, and growing with the work I do, then I will stop and formulate something from the experience to share with you, in a manner that further encourages your Trueness.

At dinner that evening, Amy looked over at me and said, "You know those things you send to us, you need to know how much we value that." What a blessing it is to hear these words from a valued relationship. The reality is, that doing work like I do, it is rare to hear such. But it is also reality that, whether it is heard or not, the impact is still there. This takes trust, a faith in the actions energized by our own Trueness, our art.

Confirming Love
While we have ample opportunities for improvement in our society, we are free. We are free to do work we love, and in our work, love others. Think about it. And where there are those who may not be readily able to take advantage of such freedom, we as leaders have a solemn accountability to create atmospheres supportive of such life-giving-sharing autonomy.

> Soul confirmation, flowing worth
> energy for the walk.
> Movement, toward relationship
> Oneness regarded.

How powerful it is to be confirmed for what you really do from the depths of who you really are. After that evening of dinner and conversation with those two true leaders, Kevin and BJ hugged, he and I shook hands, Amy and BJ hugged, and as Amy and I embraced in an appreciative hug, I said, "I love you."

It was not an accident. I spoke from the center of my soul.

So, if we work together, will I tell you I love you? Maybe. Maybe not. But one thing I will promise you, I *will* love you.

What if?

You are different from me.
Such observation begins within.
Thought often turns into statement.
And if behind the statement, fear,
the consequence on the other,
judgment.

In such judgment
is tragedy twofold:
Violence, in the direction
of the other, projected.
Violence, in the direction
of one's self, absorbed.

Allowing such violence,
projected and absorbed,
one spreads yet another layer
over the blindness
continuing to separate us
one from another.

But, what if ...

We are different; Yes!
In such exclamation,
might our eyes open
to see,
not so much, difference,
but the uniqueness
yours
mine
and the fresh oneness
created
each time
we choose to see?

Allowing Uninhibited Flow

Like Amy, Jack, Kevin, and so many others with whom I'm blessed to work, your voice—identified and consciously engaged—is your brand of love. Behind that voice, in the foundation of your Trueness, is strength. When voice is resonant and flowing, the strength behind your voice engages; it is that something you cannot help but do.

Just one week before writing this, I boarded a plane for Los Angeles to work with a client and her leadership team. Being a long flight from Ohio to California, I decided to treat myself to first class accommodations. I took my assigned seat and had barely spoken to the man next to me when he asked if I would change with his buddy a few rows forward. I agreed and moved.

No sooner than I settled into the new seat, for some reason, the man who asked me to move got bumped from his seat. I'm thinking what a waste of effort, until Brian greets me.

While your voice, however you identify or label it, is your brand of love, I actually identify my own voice as *love* itself. The strength of my voice is *encouragement*. When in the presence of another, with my voice in the freedom of flow, I simply cannot help but find some moment of encouragement for the other within what I'm hearing.

As part of his greeting, Brian asked me what I do. Upon telling him that I build confident leaders, he began telling me about his destination in New Mexico and the purpose of his travel. Brian currently works with a large company in the aircraft industry. He supports the sales force as a subject matter expert around a particular product—a product he invented and patented. After creating his innovative and very needed product, he began his own company selling directly to the end user. His frustrations with having to be too deeply involved with his sales force led him to the current position. Now, the frustrations within a large, complex organization, where his product is one of 14,000, were forcing him to consider going back to where he began.

As I listened, and offered some tactical considerations, I was waiting for the deeper issue to surface. As Brian talked about going back to where it all began, it seems his current state was a lack of passion, unlike the original desire that began it all. This can too often be the case for freelance types; he/she begins with a unique focus and purpose, only to be devastatingly distracted into the minutiae of so-called growth and success.

As Brian seemed determined to recreate a connected and passionate sales force, my encouragement took a tactical and specific approach. I shared with him the concept of interviewing for behaviors, using the power of prompting stories from the interviewee. As this captured his attention, and seemed to encourage him, I told him I would send him something on the topic when I landed. I did.

The Quiet Flow of Passion
My time with Brian was on the shorter of the two flights on the way to California. He shared quite a bit of information with me before I got to the narrowly focused encouragement. In the hopes of maybe getting a chance to be more thorough in encouraging him, I gave him my business card. Time will tell. And as I have his contact information, it's highly likely, from what I experience in this work I love, that I will think of him and send something more.

Often when meeting someone new and engaging in deep conversation, the other person acknowledges the passion in my speaking. This makes me happy, because I love what I do and it pleases me when it shows. As psychologist Mihaly Csikszentmihalyi postulates from his research and studies, while I might not be necessarily conscious of happiness while working, being in flow with what it is that I do results in my being happy. Having worked with many individuals like those about whom I tell stories, I've been blessed with the hours and experiences that have built my expertise, allowing me uninhibited flow and joyful presence in the quiet of my passion.

Whatever your deepest passion may be, it originates at the core of your voice; and within that core is the strength of voice that makes it resonant in a needy world. From this quiet core, a voice is born and grows in desire to find its impact in the world. The impact you intend is also born in this original passion. Leading from passion, the leader compels others to action within the larger flow—a story honoring oneness.

In my own life and living, my passion was foundational in developing my purpose. Living purposefully continually informs my presence. And now passion, purpose, and presence work together and move me ever closer toward oneness, clearing the lens for more wonder in the seeing.

It is difficult to *see the unfolding* if we haven't learned to see *in* the unfolding story. To develop such sight, we must engage and connect to the larger story. We must step into the flow, individually and together. It was such story-building that had called me to California.

See the Unfolding

There is work, and there is work one is called to do. Or, is it; there is work, and we are called to be who we are? It is, maybe, both/and. No matter what, under most circumstances, we are free to bring our Trueness to the doing of our work.

In the rhythm of life and living, and the balance of Wade, Walk, Wonder, if we do not allow Trueness application in the doing of a work, then the grace given to us will not flow through that work to another. To lead from original passion is to hold the tension in the eddy of enthusiasm and suffering—the reality of the passion paradox.

I was excited to arrive in California and work with Jamie and her leadership team. A recent survey in the larger organization had delivered some concerning results around how much individuals felt engaged (lack of engagement is a form of suffering in our journey with work). While this engagement concern was not the main reason for bringing her team together, it was not far from Jamie's thinking. She had been newly promoted from the peer ranks of those attending this session, and she wanted a powerful beginning of their work together, and a new, more energized focus than had previously existed.

In preparing for this session, I was impressed with, and encouraged by, Jamie's passion. Her immediate boss had provided me with a synopsis of strengths she had exhibited in her role prior to the promotion. She had diligently focused on execution and tactics, and he believed in her ability at the strategic level of purpose, to set the stage for a level of engagement leading to more meaningful application and execution.

Jamie had pulled her team together for the purpose of creating oneness around the story they desire to tell, individually and together, with the intention of bringing more meaning to application and execution. To kick off this section of the session, I asked Jamie to share her vision of the future state, in any form she wished. She opened her portfolio to her prepared comments and spoke them from her heart.

Seeing in the Clarity of Love

Jamie's love for her work, and those she is privileged to love in doing the work, came through in both message and action. After sharing her vision of the future state of the territory for which she and her team had accountability, she left the room and asked me to facilitate a dialogue of response. After about two minutes of fumbling with what they thought they were supposed to do, they looked at me and said, "We are good with what Jamie said." I loved it! I got up and went to fetch her.

Jamie is taking accountability born within her passion to create an atmosphere supportive of life-giving-sharing autonomy. From her engaging vision, the team pulled together around the story they collectively desire to tell and created clear strategies for acting on individual and shared passion. Time will tell. The story will unfold.

To *see the unfolding* we must pay attention. We must pay attention from the clarity of love. We are not focused on some distant outcome as much as we are paying attention within the present moment for the sake of how we must behave, individually and together—exhibiting faith and trust in the unfolding.

In my work, and in the life of my work, I pray I've brought my true self into play. For the most part, I believe I have. I've tried to find meaning in, and bring meaning to, the work I've been given through the years. In some instances, it may have been close to survival, but it has mostly been an approach of meaning. This is built into my wiring, deeply ingrained in my established value system.

Jamie's voice was clearly engaged as she shared her vision. The strength of her voice was leveraged in her presence with her team. Trueness was in play. She was in the flow of her passion, purpose, and presence.

Now is the Time

Do not be distracted
from the peace,
from the presence
that is yours to hold,
that is yours to let go
into your life
into your living,
into a world
grasping for peace
misunderstanding presence.

For to know presence is to know God.
For to know God is to know presence.

We can only love
in the now.
Now is the time
to love.

It is love that saves us,
always has been,
always will be.

Trueness is Participation

Since the beginning, Oneness was programed in the heart; and as such, Trueness calls the mind into the heart. And in this flow, you now feel, hear, and see reality.

Wade in this Truth

Walk with this Truth

Wonder at this Truth

Index of Poems

Trueness	1
From the Beginning	4
Simplicity, Reality, and Love	8
And Now ...	18
A brother I have (vignette)	25
Washed into the Open	28-29
Trueness Meets the World	34
Unconjectured	44
The Rhythm of Paradox	46
The View from Here	55
A Heart of Wonder	60-61
Soul confirmation (vignette)	69
What if?	70
Now is the Time	79

Continually Inspired in the Gathering

Brunson, Jeff. *Wading the Stream of Awareness: The Building of a Confident Leader.* Jonesborough: BasicApproach 2010, Stow: Soul Publishing Group, 2017.

___. *The Rhythm of Trueness: A Poetic Journey for the Leader Within.* Stow: Soul Publishing Group, 2016.

___. *In the Middle with Trueness: The Transforming Resonance of a Leader.* Jonesborough: Stow: Soul Publishing Group, 2017.

___. *The World Needs You: Selected Verse; Contemplation, Poetry, Love.* Stow: Soul Publishing Group, 2017.

Csikzentmihayli, Mihaly. *Flow: the Psychology of Optimal Experience.* New York: HarperPerennial, 2008.

Covey, Stephen R. *The 7 Habits of Highly Effective People*: New York: Simon and Schuster, 1989.

Johnson, Robert *Owning Your Own Shadow: Understanding the Dark Side of the Psyche.* New York: HarperCollins, 1991.

Palmer, Parker J. *The Promise of Paradox: A Celebration of Contradictions in the Christian Life.* San Francisco: Jossey-Bass, 2008.

Porrata, Mayra. Educator, Author, Speaker, Publisher, Community-builder. MayraPorrata.com – Bath, OH: Copyright © 2017 Mayra Porrata.

Rohr, Richard. *A Lever and a Place to Stand: The Contemplative Stance, The Active Prayer.* Mahwah: HiddenSpring, 2011.

___. *Everything Belongs: The Gift of Contemplative Prayer.* New York: Crossroad, 1999.

___. *Immortal Diamond: The Search for Our True Self.* San Francisco: Jossey-Bass, 2013.

Whyte, David. *Crossing the Unknown Sea: Work as a Pilgrimage of Identity.* New York: Riverhead Books, 2001.

___. *The Heart Aroused: Poetry and the Preservation of the Soul in Corporate America.* New York: Doubleday, 1994.

___. *The Three Marriages: Reimagining Work, Self and Relationship.* New York: Riverhead Books, 2009.

www.ingramcontent.com/pod-product-compliance
Lightning Source LLC
Chambersburg PA
CBHW020453220526
45464CB00002B/972